Liberation theology

Coming of age?

Ian Linden, CIIR

This Comment is the product of widespread consultation with,
and input from, theologians and church workers
whose invaluable contribution CIIR would like to acknowledge.

Contents

Introduction

Liberation theology arose in the turbulent 1960s, in the wake of the Second Vatican Council, which brought together the world's bishops and opened the way for the Catholic church to become more engaged with the modern world. In the Catholic cultures where it quickly took root, principally in Latin America, liberation theology became a threat to the foreign policy of the United States. It proclaimed a concept of development that challenged the power of élites and stressed the importance of people being in control of their own destiny. This stood against President JF Kennedy's development plan for Latin America, the Alliance for Progress, which championed foreign control of wealth and espoused a trickle-down approach of economic benefits to the poor.

Liberation theology refused to accept poverty as the inevitable by-product of 'progress', a prelude to rewards waiting in heaven. Instead, it was about clearing the ground for new and more radical possibilities for human development than those imposed by the structures, interests and values of US developmentalism. Its intimations of the Reign of God on earth, its insistence on changing an unjust world and not simply coping with it, mobilised countless numbers of the poor whose social awareness had previously been shaped by a more politically passive Christianity.

During the 1970s and 1980s, liberation theology was international news. It was a powerful force which both secular leaders and the Vatican tried to contain, to a point where Rome issued two authoritative 'instructions' on the topic. A policy group close to President Reagan, the Committee of Santa Fé, advised in 1980:

> US policy must begin to counter (not react against) liberation theology as it is utilised in Latin America by the 'liberation theology' clergy.

When William Casey, the Catholic director of the CIA, met with Pope John Paul II in the 1980s to discuss Poland, the Latin American church was also on the agenda.

In this Cold War context, and in the aftermath of Fidel Castro's guerrilla success in Cuba, the opponents of liberation theology conducted a propaganda campaign to project it as the bastard offspring of Christianity and Marxism, as communist infiltration of the Church. So the disintegration of the Soviet Union in the late 1980s, the fall of the Berlin Wall and the electoral defeat of the leftist Sandinista government in Nicaragua were together proclaimed as the last nails in liberation theology's coffin.

'The fall of the European governmental systems based on Marxism turned out to be a kind of twilight of the gods for that theology', the Vatican's doctrinal watchdog, Cardinal Joseph Ratzinger told specialists in Catholic doctrine in Guadalajara, Mexico, in May 1996.

Today, with liberation theology no longer newsworthy and its obituary prematurely written by its enemies, the time seems right to take stock and ask what happened to liberation theology and where it is going. Has liberation theology come of age? This *Comment* attempts to answer these questions.

What is liberation theology?

Liberation theology grew out of the faith, struggles, sufferings and hopes of the poor. It is an attempt, primarily by the poor themselves, to reflect in a religious way on their experience of poverty and injustice. This raises questions such as 'What is God doing?' and 'How is God offering salvation?' It is thus a theology that starts out in a particular political context and set of social conditions − those of the Catholic faith and the poor in Latin America − and goes on to formulate a critique that challenges both society and church.

Described as a religious reflection, liberation theology might sound like a passive activity. It is the opposite: the engagement of faith with a way of life in a cycle of action-reflection-action. Indeed, the term often used is 'doing theology'. Knowledge of God is sought through a critical reflection on praxis, the action and practice of the poor in seeking their liberation from every kind of oppression.

Political theology

Because liberation theology originated − and remains − at the intersection of contested political and religious goals, a universally acceptable definition is difficult to find. Some theologians would deny that the utterances of theology might be subject to social conditions or have a political content. At most they would agree that theological truths have implications and consequences in the realm of the political. Catholic social teaching, an organic tradition dating back to the 1890s and concerned with the principles governing political and socio-economic systems, would fall into this category. Anything more is denounced as the 'politicisation' of theology.

Liberation theologians would reply that to accept theology as valid only if it is apolitical requires self-deceit and is itself a political position providing covert support for the status quo. They would claim that this stance deprives the poor of a critical, religious voice and results in support for conservative politics.

The option for the poor

Because liberation theology in the 1970s grew from the faith of the poor, its radical Christian commitment and orientation came to be known as the 'option for the poor'. This meant, first and foremost, the engagement of the poor in their own personal, socio-economic and political liberation. In the same sense, liberation theology is accountable to the poor, and to the church as the people of God, rather than to any school of theologians or the international academic community.

Nonetheless, the 'option for the poor' also describes the religious commitment and evangelical bias of all who take the side of the poor in the quest for liberation. In the eyes of Christian faith, it is none other than God's own option. This is why the standpoint of the poor is sometimes described as theologically 'privileged'; in other words, the poor are best placed to discover and contemplate God's hidden presence in the world. It is also why liberation theology is associated with a form of spirituality that has profoundly informed the life of the churches.

The option for the poor must therefore be seen as the first priority. Doing theology from this perspective comes second, like writing a thoughtful and prayerful diary about work in progress. But it is an important and influential second. The Peruvian theologian, Gustavo Gutiérrez, one of the early fathers of liberation theology, took as his starting point the profoundly practical missionary question: 'How is it possible to tell the poor, who are forced to live in conditions that embody a denial of love, that God loves them?'[1] He implied that this message would be a lie if God's love, and thus the Christian gospel, were not about changing the world of the poor economically, socially and politically.

Prophetic theology

The option for the poor and its accompanying theology have motivated and underpinned the work of countless Christians in community development, trades unions, economic research aimed at challenging the status quo, political parties of the left, liberation movements and national democratic struggles, particularly in Latin America, southern Africa and parts of Asia, and, for a few, in Europe and North America. It has qualified many for torture, imprisonment and sometimes death. Above all it has generated a spirituality that strengthened Christian participation in processes of — usually secular — transformation, and allowed many to take part in radical action by liberating them from oppressive forms of religious practice.

That is why liberation theology should be seen as one of several prophetic theologies, alongside feminist theology, black theology, cultural theologies and eco-theology. These all, in their different contexts, share the urge to respond to the same divine demand for doing justice, to the believer's discovery of what is wrong and needs putting right.

Liberation theology has been historically significant in its provision of a Christian witness to the option for the poor. Moreover, it has sponsored a distinctive spirituality. It does not ask to be judged by any other mission than this; nor, perhaps, ought it to be.

Origins of liberation theology

There are specific reasons why Latin America in the 1960s should have provided the seed-bed for liberation theology. The conditions in the region help to account for some of the features of liberation theology that may be less relevant to other times and places.

The continent was in ferment. Brazil had undergone a military coup in 1964 that unleashed a wave of brutality. Cuba had become the front line in the Cold War, the symbol of revolution. Catholic organisations such as Catholic Action in Brazil, and even the usually conservative Legion of Mary in Uruguay, were soon to see their members pulled into radical political action and, sometimes, guerrilla warfare. The ferment extended to student circles where the Marxist writings of figures such as Anibel Ponce in Argentina, José Carlos Mariategui in Peru and Farabundo Martí in El Salvador were discussed, as were 'underdevelopment' theories of poverty (the idea that development as a process in the North engendered exploitation and stagnation of economies in the South).

In many parts of Latin America — the most extensive development and organisation being in Brazil — base Christian communities (BCCs) grew up from the late 1950s onwards. They were rooted in discussion and communal reflection on the scriptures and the lived reality of the communities, mutual help, prayer and adult education. Often led by lay ministers known as 'delegates of the Word', the BCCs were formed in poor areas on the urban fringe and in rural parishes, originally as a response to a shortage of priests. Compared to the total number of Catholics on parish registers, the numbers were small: their membership achieved at most

8   *CIIR Comment*

two to five per cent of the church-going Christian community during the 1980s, the period of the BCCs' most rapid expansion. Nor were their members the poorest of the poor, who, through hunger and debility, were unable to sustain long meetings nor could see in the BCCs an answer to their immediate material needs.

Nonetheless the BCCs were the crucible in which a new way of 'being church' was forged. Here the insights of liberation theology were generated and sustained by concrete action. If the unity of theory and practice meant by the term 'praxis' found purchase in a lived Christian reality, it was within the life of the BCCs. It was among people who had a stake in both society and church, however little, however much from the underside.

BCCs were not revolutionary cells. But among them were people — often young — whose education and capacity for social analysis led them to take radical social action to right local wrongs, not simply to alleviate poverty but sometimes to challenge the structures that reinforced it.

In retrospect the BCCs may seem a harmless structural innovation in Latin American church life, but some perceived

---

Destruction of Solentiname

The 1970s were a time of steady expansion of base Christian communities in several countries. Perhaps the best known became those on the archipelago in Lake Nicaragua which formed the basis for Father Ernesto Cardenal's *The Gospel in Solentiname*, a book reflecting the direct application of the methods of liberation theology among the peasants.

This community was later to be attacked and razed by President Anastasio Somoza's National Guard (thereby supplying new recruits, including Father Cardenal, for the Sandinista movement).

---

them to be a political threat. This led to divisions in the church. The BCCs, radical priests, the Sisters and lay organisations involved came to be known as the 'Church of the Poor' – a shorthand description that points to the faultline running through the church. It was these changes within the church, and the implications they held for hierarchical control, as much as liberation theology's advocacy of radical social transformation, that eventually caused alarm bells to ring in the Vatican. Some conservatives saw the changes as redolent of Protestantism. In reality, these reactions to a large extent reflected a church of the powerful closing ranks against a challenge to its power.

From the Second Vatican Council to Medellín

Another future rift between Rome and sectors of the Latin American church could have been glimpsed during the Second Vatican Council (1962-65), despite its opening up of the church to contemporary socio-economic and political issues. With the exception of interventions by the saintly Archbishop of Recife in Brazil, Dom Helder Camara, and the small 'Church of the Poor' group of bishops to which he belonged, Latin American theological themes made little impact on the conciliar bishops. The Council, one of the most important church gatherings for centuries, was carried forward by the logic of a creative school of European — particularly French — theological thought.

It is true that there was some convergence: in Latin America, Pope John XXIII's commendation of the movements of workers and women and his *apertura a sinistra* ('opening to the left') gave heart, as did his anti-racism. Likewise, Pope Paul VI's historic 1967 encyclical, *The Progress of Peoples*, critically analysed themes of world justice, development and peace. But the spark which had already ignited the tinder of liberation theology was the Latin American continent's gross social and economic inequality and injustice.

Between 1964 and 1965 four meetings of predominantly Catholic theologians took place — in Bogotá (Colombia), Cuernavaca (Mexico), Havana (Cuba) and Petropolis (Brazil). Participants achieved a new consensus, agreeing that the times called for an 'historic theology'. This should include a narrative of domination and oppression and so seek to talk about God in the history of the poor and downtrodden.

In 1966 the Latin American Episcopal Council (CELAM), a coordinating body for the Catholic church in Latin America, met in Mar del Plata, Argentina. Dom Helder Camara addressed the question of underdevelopment and called for 'structural transformation' as its antidote. At the next annual CELAM meeting, which also echoed the themes of *The Progress of Peoples*, a commitment was made to formulate a pastoral strategy that would reflect its insights and priorities. This led to the second general conference of the bishops of Latin America, at Medellín, Colombia, in 1968.

The 130 bishops and archbishops gathered at Medellín placed themselves firmly on the side of the continent's poor and undertook a sustained critique of Latin American society. They also, in effect, endorsed a commitment to a 'poor church' that adopted poverty as 'the condition of the needy of the world in order to bear witness to the evil that it represents.'[2] They thereby set the Spanish and Latin American tradition, which focused on the sufferings of Christ on the Cross, in the context of a struggle against evil rather than a fatalistic contemplation of the inevitable:

> We, the bishops, wish to come closer to the poor in sincerity and brotherhood, making ourselves accessible to them. We ought to sharpen the awareness of our duty of solidarity with the poor to which charity leads us. This solidarity means that we make ours their problems and their struggles [. . .] This has to be concretised in

criticism of injustice and oppression, in the struggle against the intolerable situation which a poor person often has to tolerate.[3]

Medellín had far-reaching influence. In both Pope Paul VI's 1971 apostolic letter, *Octogesima Adveniens*, and in the 1971 synod of bishops' endorsement that work for justice was a constitutive dimension of evangelisation, the pastoral concerns of Medellín were apparent.

Medellín's central theme, picked up later by Latin American theologians, was one of captivity and exile; the poor were caught in an alien economic and political system on the biblical model of the Israelites in Egypt. The pastoral task of evangelisation thus had 'education for liberation' as a priority. This concept, taken from the popular Brazilian educator, the late Paolo Freire, meant the 'conscientisation' of the poor, building an awareness of the possibility of change. The BCCs were to be a privileged forum for this process.

This was not the only theme circulating in the Latin American church. For many in the Christians for Socialism movement in Chile, founded after socialist Salvador Allende's coalition came to power in 1970, a radical reading of the Bible demanded Christians' commitment to a socialist political project. But for those who would not be so politically explicit, it necessarily involved at least a struggle against underdevelopment. In the three years after Medellín the momentum of theological debate increased, feeding on the growing political crisis in Latin America.

This was the context in which the Peruvian, Gustavo Gutiérrez, chaplain to the National Union of Catholic Students and professor at the Catholic University in Lima, began to synthesise the central preoccupations of the Christian community around him with those of the wider school of radical Latin American theologians. The first major liberation theology texts followed. In 1971 Gutiérrez published a scholarly work, *Teología de la Liberación* ('A Theology of Liberation'), in Lima. The name of the book became the name not simply of a school of theology but of an international movement in the Catholic church. Soon after Gutiérrez's study, the Brazilian Leonardo Boff published *Jesucristo Liberador* ('Jesus Christ Liberator'), a book different in emphasis but similar in its new methodology. A year later, in 1973, the Society of Jesus, led by its Superior General Pedro Arrupe, formally adopted the theme 'Faith that does Justice' and, a decade later, the option for the poor as the hallmark of Jesuit life.

From Medellín to Santo Domingo: the counter-attack

By the time people were reading Gutiérrez and Boff, reaction had already set in. Spearheaded by Alfonso López Trujillo, auxiliary bishop of Bogotá, the regional 'counter-reformation' established its opposition in the periodical *Tierra Nueva* in 1972. This was published by a Belgian Jesuit, Roger Vekemans, who had been a conduit for the CIA in sponsoring the cause of Christian democracy in Chile. Allende's electoral victory in Chile in 1970 had provoked growing conflict in the Catholic church. Behind this lay the fear that liberation theology might be turning the church into an instrument for a socialist/Marxist political project. Anxiety about the political content of liberation theology and its social analysis spread among Latin American bishops, making them more vulnerable to manipulation by the political right.

Their anxieties were fuelled by the writings of, for example, Gutiérrez, who said that all analysis of underdevelopment should be placed in the framework of 'the worldwide class struggle between rich and poor'. However, specific advocacy of socialism as a political ideology was missing from Boff's early writings. Moreover, Juan Luis Segundo, another of the founding fathers, explicitly ruled out politics dominated by ideology. Liberation theologians tended not to specify support for any particular political project, placing their emphasis rather on the coming Reign of God. Marxist vocabulary, when it was used, described and analysed the conflicts of interest that any empirical study of land ownership, human rights, militarism and the power of the oligarchies in the Latin American countries would have revealed. This approach was distinct from the explicitly socialist political emphasis of Christians for Socialism in Chile. However, the differences were deliberately blurred in the López Trujillo-Vekemans onslaught.

It is true that liberation theology was later diminished as a witness to the option for the poor by its imprecise and inadequate social analysis. Underdevelopment theory was soon to be discounted and Marxist insights into the role of the peasantry, who were the vast majority of the poor, were often notably absent. However, this was not the problem that the conservatives had with liberation theology. Their problem was about power in church and society. Marxism was a convenient stick with which to beat the radicals. In reality, a contextual theology of and for the poor threatened conservatives' control over ideas, church structures and the many compromises that the church had made with an unjust political system. Furthermore, as they saw it — and there was no lack of sincerity in the conservative backlash — the spiritual was being polluted, not renewed, by the political content of liberation theology.

The battle lines were firmly drawn by the time CELAM met at Sucre, Bolivia, in November 1972. Bishop López Trujillo had carefully prepared the ground. He was elected secretary-general and conservatives took over key departments for the laity and for social action. As López Trujillo concentrated power in Bogotá, elections to the CELAM structures were henceforth to be a focus of the conflict in the Latin American church between those who championed an option for the poor and its theology, and those who opposed it.

Intensified repression

The tide of history in the late 1970s, however, was running with the liberation theologians' vision of the need for radical change. Debt repayments were soon crippling national economies and the standard of living for ordinary Latin Americans went into free fall. Military dictatorships in Bolivia, Uruguay, Chile and Argentina, together with right-wing regimes in other Latin American countries, imposed fierce military repression on organisations of the poor. The National Security State was not a figment of theological imagination: it was a well-elaborated strategy for domination which killed, among its many victims, scores of priests, nuns, catechists and local church leaders as they fought for basic human rights throughout the continent.[4] It did so with the complicity or transparent support of the government of the United States.

If Marxist social analysis had not been ready to hand, the conditions of Latin America might have pushed liberation theologians with any respect for their local reality to invent it. The 1970s dreams of *el pueblo unido* ('the people united'), the revolutionary slogan which identified the poor as the new subjects of history united in a struggle for liberation, seemed no more fantastic than the false promises of development and a New Economic Order inherited from the optimism of the 1960s.

Puebla conference

The third General Conference of the Latin American bishops, scheduled for Puebla in 1978 but delayed until 1979 because of the death of two Popes, Paul VI and John Paul I, was intended to be the final ambush in the conservatives' strategy. It almost backfired. This was partly a result of the growing consensus among pastorally-oriented Latin American bishops that poverty, and the political conflicts it engendered, were a greater enemy than liberation theology. It was also a result of tactical blunders by López Trujillo. First among these was his publication of the conference's preparatory working paper in December 1977.

So little did the 'Green Book', as it was dubbed, speak to the condition of the Latin American church that it was effectively thrown out. But before this happened it created a ferment in church communities and sparked a continent-wide consultative process. The vast majority of the bishops, whose preoccupations were the pastoral care of their communities, thus went to Puebla with an acute awareness of the continent's human rights violations and a reluctance to condemn Christians who were organising against them. They spoke of the needs of the poor, the rights of indigenous peoples and the oppression of women.

The language of the Puebla final document, published in 1979, clearly attempts to substitute different formulations for the phrases and key words of the liberation theologians. But no other sentence highlights the failure of the conservative minority better than the one which was to live on in the language of solidarity throughout the world:

> We affirm the need for conversion on the part of the whole church to a preferential option for the poor, an option aimed at their integral liberation.[5]

The partial failure of the conservatives at Puebla proved only a temporary setback. López Trujillo rose to become President of CELAM and, later, a Cardinal. Pope John Paul II, for whom Puebla was the first major engagement of his pontificate, denounced the 'politicisation of the person of Jesus'. He was soon in open conflict with the 'Sandinista' clergy in Nicaragua, whose political commitment had been strongly influenced by liberation theology. The Pope's east European background predisposed him to sympathise with all who could convince him that what conservatives regarded as the virus of communism was infecting the Latin American church.

Theological dialogue
In September 1984, the Congregation for the Doctrine of the Faith, the Vatican's doctrinal watchdog, produced its first instruction on liberation theology. Written under the direction of Cardinal Joseph Ratzinger (who, ironically, had supervised Leonardo Boff's early theological studies in Munich), it had the tone of a professor admonishing an unruly student, a lofty condescension that seemed to come from Europe's oak-panelled libraries, hermetically sealed against the idiom and clamour of Latin America's shantytowns. Nonetheless, the *Instruction on Certain Aspects of the Theology of Liberation*[6] marshalled a number of theological criticisms which would, and did, weigh with 'pastoral' bishops who were uncertain in their judgement.

At the same time, Leonardo Boff was required to go to Rome in person to answer charges arising from his book *Church: Charism and Power*,[7] an attack on authoritarianism which offered a radical vision of what the church needed to be if it were to become the church of the poor. He was accompanied by his fellow Brazilian Franciscans, Cardinals Paolo Arns and Aloisio Lorscheider. The fact that in attacking Boff the Congregation was taking on two distinguished and widely respected church leaders and with them, implicitly, a significant part of the enormous Brazilian church, did not pass unnoticed at the Vatican.

Boff was temporarily silenced but the dialogue proved cathartic. The Vatican's subsequent *Instruction on Christian Freedom and Liberation,*[8] published in March 1986, adopted a more sympathetic tone. It rarely mentioned liberation theology directly, portraying it as a necessary response to the conditions of injustice around the world and describing BCCs as 'a source of great hope for the Church'. The tone was carefully nuanced, showing clear signs of the Pope's own interventions and demonstrating understanding for the plight of the poor, while warning against 'excesses'. By this was meant any suggestion that 'redemption' was a political process, that liberation required Marxist philosophy as its essential guideline, and anything that brought priests into leadership roles in radical political parties.

This second instruction was followed by a special meeting with the Brazilian bishops. In his letter to them, the Pope argued that liberation theology 'must constitute a new stage — intimately connected with those that have gone before — of the theological reflection.'[9] He saw such a theology of liberation as 'correct and necessary'. In one sense, Rome had moved. In another, the position amounted to a stand-off.

A stand-off meant war by other means: the second instruction, that of March 1986, opened a period of attrition around ecclesiastical preferment. Rome replaced retiring bishops believed to be tainted by liberation theology with men who would not rock the boat. The Vatican sometimes got it wrong, as it had done most spectacularly before, in the 1970s, with Archbishop Oscar Romero in El Salvador. Those who translated their commitment to a preferential option for the poor into support for radical action were kept under special scrutiny. Cardinal Arns, whose pastoral action in Sao Paolo was a direct translation of the option for the poor, saw his archdiocese broken up in the 1990s.

By the time the Latin American bishops met for their fourth great continent-wide conference at Santo Domingo in 1992, there had been as much initial skirmishing as before Puebla. But time had moved on. The end of the Cold War, the defeat of the Sandinista government and the sense of failure among the Latin American left at not having gained power, had intervened. The BCCs no longer expected imminent change, however well organised they had become at a national level (as in Brazil). Some were reduced to little more than informal groups meeting irregularly. Many had lost key members to political parties, where they made significant contributions. Although the problems of poverty and injustice were unchanged — indeed they were exacerbated by neo-liberal economic policies — the Vatican was now dancing on the grave of communism. The terrain on which liberation theologians clashed with conservatives had shifted irrevocably.

Most notably, at Santo Domingo the 'centre' of the Latin American church gravitated to the question of local culture. This was in opposition to what were perceived as attempts by Rome to impose a European 'Christian culture' that ignored the reality of indigenous communities and the changing life of Latin America's vast cities. Equally to the fore of conference discussion were the urgent need for land reform and the rural problems created by neo-liberalism. Liberation theologians tactfully kept their distance from the conference for fear of creating a backlash.

Interpretations of the Santo Domingo conference varied according to the expectations that it had aroused. For many Latin American Christians, who had feared a dangerous rolling-back of pastoral options for the poor, it was a relative success in that they had held their ground. Rome had learnt little from Puebla and, heavy-handed and manipulative, had rallied most pastorally-minded bishops against itself again.

However, for those who remembered liberation theologians as the movers and shakers of two decades before, it looked as if an historic project had lost its hold on the decision-makers and leaders of the Latin American church.

Both views, in a sense, missed the point. Liberation theology had spread globally and, although inevitably diluted, had entered the mainstream of church thinking.

Santo Domingo
The New Signs of the Times in the Realm of Human Development

Pastoral Directions
• Promote a change of attitude on the value of land on the basis of the Christian world view, which has connections with the cultural traditions of the poor and small farmers.

• Remind the lay faithful that they must influence the agrarian policies of their governments (especially their modernisation policies) and peasant and indigenous organizations, so as to attain ways of using the land that are just, most community-oriented, and participatory.

• Support all those persons and institutions striving to bring governments and those who own the means of production to create a just and humane agrarian reform policy, one that can legislate, plan, and provide support for a more just distribution of land and for utilizing it more efficiently.

• Support in solidarity those organizations of small farmers and indigenous people who are struggling through just and legitimate channels to hold on to or reacquire their lands.

From *Santo Domingo Conclusions*, CIIR/CAFOD, London, 1993.

Global spread

Before 1974, outside the religious orders whose general chapters brought together members from around the world, there were few opportunities for Latin American liberation theologians to influence their colleagues in Africa and Asia. Cross-fertilisation of ideas was at first limited to a select Spanish-speaking few. However, some Christian communities — for example in the Philippines — were independently reflecting on their specific context, 'doing theology', developing BCCs and thus using the methods of liberation theology.

In the United States, the first key channel for liberation theology was the Catholic Interamerican Cooperation Programme (CICOP), part of the US Catholic Conference. However, it was subject to the US bishops and its dynamic director, Louis Colonese, was removed and CICOP subsequently disbanded. Nonetheless, by the end of 1973 a Catholic publishing house, Orbis, had brought out Gustavo Gutiérrez's seminal study, *A Theology of Liberation*, in English and liberation theology texts were beginning to circulate throughout the anglophone world. An international meeting of theologians in Detroit in 1975, 'Theology in the Americas', was a turning point. It was followed a year later in Dar-es-Salaam by the setting up of the Ecumenical Association of Third World Theologians (EATWOT). This was to become an important vehicle for transmitting debate and discussion around the world, and between different religions.

The Latin American themes of poverty, inequality and repression appealed particularly to Christians living in similar situations elsewhere. Such ills did not disappear during the intensification of the Cold War in the 1980s. Indeed, they had become more acute in the shape of 'low intensity conflict', a violent form of counter-insurgency. Many died because of their faith commitment and were seen as martyrs in the struggle for justice. Theologians such as the Jesuit Jon Sobrino in El Salvador wove this experience of the suffering and martyrdom of the poor, oppressed and marginalised into their understanding of Christian spirituality.

The rise of contextual theologies

South Africa's apartheid regime, the Marcos dictatorship in the Philippines and, to a lesser extent, the Korean regimes and the Indian caste system all proved in different ways a forcing-ground for local contextual theologies. These found resonance in what Latin Americans were writing and talking about.

The Philippines was in many ways closest to the Latin American experience but political imperatives dominated. A large movement, Christians for National Liberation, formed part of the National Democratic Front (NDF), which included (and was dominated by) the Communist Party. Christians for National Liberation largely neglected the elaboration of a locally rooted theology and drew on an eclectic, although principally Maoist, social and political analysis. Nonetheless, owing to the common relationship with the United States, Latin American liberation theology was read avidly in radical Filipino religious groups, while the option for the poor, particularly among certain religious orders, informed pastoral practice from the 1970s onwards. This drew Christians into conflict with the military, landowners and, as environmental concerns grew, loggers.

South African radicals, although fascinated by the Sandinista revolution and Latin America, developed more of a local theology. In September 1985, 151 Christians published

Archbishop Oscar Romero

The archetypal figurehead for radical Christian commitment to the poor was Archbishop Oscar Romero of San Salvador. Romero stood for countless poor in his own country, but also for others, such as the thousands of indigenous people massacred in Guatemala's killing fields. Romero's assassination, on 24 March 1980, a few weeks after he had written to President Carter asking him not to send military aid to El Salvador, and the day after he had appealed to the Salvadorean soldiers to stop their killing, was the predictable end of a prophetic ministry in Latin America. He was murdered at the instigation of the Salvadorean military. The Word of God uttered as good news for the poor qualified its interlocutor for prison, torture or death.

The Kairos Document, a theological comment on the political crisis. 'Kairos' is 'the moment of grace and opportunity, the favourable time in which God issues a challenge to decisive action'. The document drew on traditional African concepts of evil, underpinned its thinking with biblical sources and offered a trenchant critique of the churches' reaction to apartheid.

Kairos theology in South Africa, Dalit theology in India (Dalits form the lowest caste), and Minjung theology in South Korea (Minjung are 'the people' or 'masses') were not exotic offshoots from a Latin American stock. They were culturally specific political theologies arising out of common experiences. South African radicals' understanding of the apartheid regime was different from South Koreans' reaction to the illegitimacy of their military dictatorship, a reaction based on the concept of *han* or 'just indignation'. But Christians in both countries were found in the worker movement, went to jail and developed a spirituality of resistance and struggle.

By the end of the 1980s, there was growing interchange and

dialogue between practitioners of different contextual theologies. Christian theologians from Latin America, South Africa and Asia came together to analyse their situation and reflect on their experience. In their pastoral ministry all were working for social justice based on an option for the poor. All had in their countries popular national democratic movements of varying strengths; all were subject to varying levels of repression. The Catholic Institute for International Relations (CIIR) provided a central administration for one such process. The resulting document, *The Road to Damascus: Kairos and Conversion*, was published simultaneously in a number of signatory countries (El Salvador, Guatemala, Nicaragua, Philippines, Korea, Namibia and South Africa) in August 1989. The Damascus document expressed in its title the call to conversion of right-wing Christians who were persecuting the Church of the Poor. Its critique of imperialism and low intensity conflict was biblical, radical and thus outspoken in tone. Some rich, powerful, but conservative German church circles sought to denounce it. However, the document was supported by the Lutheran church in Norway and found favour in the World Council of Churches, which disseminated it widely.

Ironically, as these diverse traditions of liberation theology from different continents were coming together in the beginnings of a global analysis and reflection, the world that they were setting out to analyse from the underside was on the brink of seismic political changes: the fall of the Berlin Wall, the collapse of bureaucratic communist government in eastern Europe, the end of the Cold War and the disintegration of the Soviet Union. The Damascus document thus appeared as a fitting epitaph to the Cold War rather than the manifesto for a new Christian internationalism to transcend it.

Radical Christian challenges to liberation theology

Despite EATWOT and shared preparations for the Damascus document, Latin American liberation theology was slow to respond to themes from other continents and cultures. There was perhaps a touch of arrogance in the assumption that others had to answer the challenge of the Latin American context and not vice versa. This risked undervaluing the achievements of some progressive academic European theology and neglecting the emphases coming from Africa and Asia. It was also liable to cause sparks to fly in international meetings of third world theologians.

Latin American Christians, of course, had not been through the experience of the black consciousness movement in the United States and South Africa, and had thus not been forced to take other cultural traditions as seriously as their own. This could be particularly annoying to African theologians in EATWOT, who responded by rejecting several Latin American theological positions, taking them to be aspects of a new intellectual colonialism.

Although the rights and importance of indigenous peoples featured in theological dispatches during the 1980s, indigenous clergy rarely represented Latin America in international conferences. The same was true of feminist theologians, whose fate at the hands of the Vatican could be no less severe (although causing less of an outcry) than that of male theologians. At the EATWOT 1982 Delhi congress, accusations that liberation theologians ignored women resulted in the forming of a women's commission.

By the end of the 1980s women and indigenous peoples were organising more effectively in both church and society and asserting their right to be heard in international fora. The 1992 Santo Domingo conference, with its emphasis on culture, was the culmination of growing awareness throughout the church, and particularly among liberation theologians, that it had neglected the experience of indigenous peoples and women. Moreover, they would have to differentiate between different categories of 'the poor'.

Gradual assimilation of liberation theology
The Santo Domingo conference was therefore something of a watershed. Liberation theology was at once evolving and disappearing from centre stage. It had become part of the theological wallpaper, not noticeable simply because those in the room were so used to it being there, yet giving the room its distinctive appearance.

The core ideas of liberation theology had spread across the world: the option for the poor and their liberation; the need to analyse the context, to read the signs of the times; the importance of historical and social analysis; the systemic and structural — not personal — nature of conflict and violence; idolatry rather than atheism as a core problem of modern society; and the rediscovery of the prophetic tradition of the Bible and of Jesus's journey in history.

Such themes, of course, are not exclusively those of liberation theology. Had they been, it would not have been seen as a necessary new stage in the development of the church's thinking, as Pope John Paul II described it in his letter to the Brazilian bishops in 1986 (see page 18). It is difficult to analyse whether and to what degree the themes of liberation theology welled up from old springs of Catholic tradition, whether they were generated out of a unique ferment in the third world church or were imported. This in itself indicates the pervasive spread and assimilation of liberation theology's methods and ideas.

Eastern Europe, the former Soviet Union and China

This spread, however, has been uneven rather than truly global. Liberation theology never took root in several significant areas. The distinctive history of oppression in eastern Europe and the Soviet Union, their isolation during the Cold War and the effective anti-communist propaganda used against liberation theologians, have all resulted in incomprehension and often open hostility to liberation theology. The way communist regimes in the Soviet Union and China brought churches under state control or suppressed them left Christians outside state-approved religious bodies acutely sensitive to any hint of a manipulative politicisation of theology. The large underground church in China and the small communities of Baptists, Catholics and Christian dissidents in the Soviet Union distrusted liberation theologians who visited and talked with communist party officials and intellectuals. They gave the worst possible interpretation to the use of Marxist vocabulary and themes attributable to communist party internationalism.

One of the major historical legacies of the Cold War was therefore a theological and spiritual divide in the Catholic church between the Christianity of Eastern Europe and the Soviet Union and that of the Third World. This was reflected in west European organisations which, with the exception of a few such as the official Catholic peace movement, Pax Christi, related to either one or the other. (The division was formally absent in the World Council of Churches and at Rome synods, even if it operated at decision-making levels.)

The west European context

The problem in western Europe was incomprehension of another sort. It was symptomatic that liberation theology first came on to the European agenda in 1972, when many key

Latin American theologians were invited to the Escorial Palace in Spain for a meeting of the Jesuit Institute of Faith and Secularity. The sumptuous venue and academic ambience showed scant understanding of how a liberation theology might develop in Europe. In the event, opponents of liberation theology quickly dismissed it as a gilded snare to be resisted with Catholic common sense. Yet the hope that liberation theology might prove a panacea for Europe's spiritual ills remained. The mistake was to imagine that liberation theology could be lifted off the peg like a bespoke suit, rather than be allowed to grow out of the lived reality of poverty and exclusion in Europe.

In Britain, which lacked the popular Catholic culture of much of Latin America, the atomisation of a secular society under neo-liberalism deprived theologians of shared meanings and accessible forms of community. The Christian faith community did not have the Italian Marxist Antonio Gramsci's category of 'organic intellectuals' in the way that Latin American liberation theologians might be seen as growing naturally from a common Catholic culture and 'base community'. A coherent 'British liberation theology' appeared either tantalisingly unattainable, because its social analysis was based on such a complex and diverse society, or else crassly derivative, because it was not. In the meantime, many of those working in situations of increasing social deprivation and economic exploitation were trying to 'do theology'. They were trying to make theological sense of their experience of the suffering, meaninglessness, and exclusion so typical of the underside of Britain since 1979, when Margaret Thatcher's conservative government came to power.

By the 1980s several new attempts at theological reflection on poverty and marginalisation in the European context were being made. This was not the first approach to prophetic theology in Europe. The German theologians Dietrich Bonhoeffer, Juergen Moltmann and Johann-Baptist Metz had already made a substantial contribution to the development of a critical political theology, forged in the aftermath of the Second World War. Yet the exclusion of the marginalised in Europe and the complexity of the system which subtly oppresses a large minority, the 'underclass', poses special problems for social analysis and mobilisation. Groups such as Kairos Europa, attempting to apply kairos theology to Europe, struggled with these special problems. Many radical European Christian groups gave particular attention to exploited immigrants, especially as neo-fascist movements were targeting and beginning to kill them. In short, the 'poor' was a term even more in need of being disaggregated in Europe than in the Third World. Meanwhile, the major innovative and influential strand of theology coming out of European and US industrial society's experience of neo-liberalism and oppression was feminist, cutting across the fundamental socio-economic distinctions of early liberation theology.

But, if liberation theology has had little impact on the mainstream churches of the North, from Galway to Vladivostok, and from Seattle to New York, it is above all because it is not rooted in the spiritual problems that preoccupy the North. The South might have expected from the topside of history something like a 'Pharaonic theology', a theology liberating societies of post-imperial rulers, to complement their own themes of exile, exodus from Egypt, and martyrdom; but a contextualised European theology found itself stricken with doubt about its capacity to do theology at all. Any narrative claiming to be a Northern historical theology would have to include the experience of catastrophic violence, anti-semitism, genocide, and the different totalitarianisms. But the unique reality of Europe, on which a distinctive spirituality might be based, inspired the equivalent of a theoretical stutter, not an articulate quest for a usable prophetic, political theology.

In short, European contextual theologies are not, and increasingly are seen not to be, the elaboration of relatively seamless and unproblematic readings of gospel texts with reference to injustice. So, while minorities experienced growing impoverishment and marginalisation, Europeans appear culturally unable to construct a theology from 'the margins'.

Today, in a world where political and economic power are becoming more and more centralised, Europe inhabits an ideological universe which is post-modern and de-centred. It disclaims grand narratives, offering instead a babel of competing voices most of which may be deemed to be 'marginal'. This is part and parcel of a philosophical climate in which relativism flourishes. Those who claim to speak only from particular positions and for special interest groups cannot easily take a stance with regard to issues of global injustice, and have scant resources for broad social and political critiques. Addressing this ideological impasse stands now as an integral part of any future European liberation theology.

Critiques of liberation theology

Liberation theology should be judged on whether it provides an adequate foundation, both theological and practical, for a religious presence in the world which acts as a witness to the preferential option for the poor. Respect for the third world church, and humility in the face of it, should not preclude asking this question. Liberation theology, like any theology, needs perennially to be tested to be sure of its liberating truth. And it is being tested from a variety of angles: feminism, ecology, the success of the evangelical churches, and a philosophical challenge to the Christian quality of liberation theology's practical politics.

So, is liberation theology up to its task and has it succeeded in carrying it out? These questions are timely in the light of the epoch-making global changes since 1989. Indeed, liberation theologians have been the first to ask them. But a sense of perspective is needed: liberation theology has been around for barely a quarter of a century. It may need to respond to intractable theological problems, such as the meaning of Christ's 'atonement' on the Cross, and the 'Reign of God', but it is hardly surprising if it has no convincing ready-made answers. Nor do schools of theology that date back centuries.

Many criticisms of liberation theology have not been made in a spirit of enquiry or out of solidarity, from within a community committed to an option for the poor. Some critics have assumed that an option for the poor can be guaranteed only by adherence to some other principle, a spiritualised understanding of salvation, which their theological formulations uniquely embody and expound, and which their particular Christian practice uniquely enacts. By this reasoning, they have no need to set their critique explicitly in the framework of fidelity to God's option for the poor. Cardinal Ratzinger's critique in the first Vatican instruction would be the classic of this genre.

The kindest interpretation of past criticisms from the Vatican is that Rome reacted instinctively to conflict in the Latin American church. It therefore articulated its anxieties in a form which failed to come to grips with the fundamental engagement of liberation theology with the poor. The two Vatican instructions, for example, either endorse an abstract, apolitical commitment to 'liberation and freedom', or attack the political project that they imagine to be at the heart of liberation theology. Either way, the documents' goals appear narrowly political: an attempt to bridle and demobilise a movement that was profoundly evangelical in its origins and basic orientation. The Vatican's policy was widely construed as defensive rather than constructive.

The 'Cambridge' critique

It is prudent to be suspicious of the Vatican's position; yet in it can be glimpsed questions about liberation theology's account of politics and the acquisition of knowledge that bear consideration. For example, didn't liberation theologians adopt too uncritically a secular concept of politics? This is a question posed by Cambridge theologians Nicholas Lash and John Milbank.

Lash's and Milbank's argument is not that liberation theology tried to baptise a particular political theory — Marxism — or that it has tried to make the church its political tool, but that its account of the political is not critical or rigorous enough. They see the liberation theologians as unwittingly taking over a definition of politics that is bound up with Nietzsche's view that the fundamental form of power is domination and its corollary, violence. The Vatican may have sensed this when it recoiled from the violence of class conflict inherent in Marxist analysis, which it believed the liberation theologians to have adopted. It failed to trace the philosophical problem back to Nietzsche's understanding of politics as 'orientation to power'.

Thus Lash's and Milbank's critique amounts to the charge that liberation theology has accepted a form of rationality that imprisons and turns persons into instruments of a universal 'will to power'. It cannot therefore propose a 'Christian politics' that would, to quote Lash, 'exhibit the peaceable generosity of God'. The politics implicitly adopted by liberation theology does not express the quality of God's power as service, love and gift. In other words, the politics of liberation theology is not at its deepest level — as a way of knowing God and the world — liberating. Liberation theology is not, in the Christian sense, political enough.

Response to Cambridge

In response, it might be argued that liberation theology has not, on the whole, attempted to promote any political dispensation as such. It has kept within the confines of prophetic denunciation of prevailing political systems. Indeed, a striking characteristic of liberation theology is its apparent lack of interest in Catholic social teaching, which sketches in rough contours the political system that Christians might seek.

Moreover, what the first liberation theologians were seeking as a Christian politics may be glimpsed in what they rejected in the politics of the day. The central themes in the 1960s and early 1970s writings of Gutiérrez, Segundo and Boff were domination and oppression in economic, social and political systems. Inasmuch as they wrote about a hoped-for political dispensation, it was essentially utopian and theological, the Reign of God. This reflected the urgency that Christians in Latin America felt about the injustice around them, an urgency based on suffering that corresponded to the kairos theme in South Africa. In both, the undercurrents of a popular Christian culture in crisis can be detected.

Given the later writings on martyrdom and the 'crucified peoples' of Central America, from Jon Sobrino, Rodolfo Cardenal and Ignacio Ellacuria, it is difficult to sustain the argument that liberation theology was in practice indifferent to a Christian account of the nature of power. In their writings, power is revealed as the strength of non-violent rejection of evil. Ultimately, the power which liberation theologians speak of as available to the Christian political community is the power of bodily absence and loss, that of Christ and the martyrs. In the mystery of Christian celebration this becomes a powerful presence and communal strength. In Latin American celebrations the cry of *presente* indicates a sense of the continuing presence of those who have died for the living community. It was partly the sense of this power, which promised to transform the absence and loss of a dead comrade into a strength, that led many communists in the South African liberation movement actively to seek Christian involvement in funerals.

Feminist criticisms

Male liberation theologians have been slow to assimilate some of feminism's insights into the dynamics of power in social structures. Feminist theologians argue that the blindness to issues of gender in early liberation theology reflects the cultural strength of patriarchy, and in particular the cult of *machismo* in Latin American society and in the church.

At another level, however, this shortcoming stemmed from the difficulty of developing a coherent political project that incorporated a critique of different forms of domination — ethnicity, gender, race and religion. This became clear when theologians began to focus on the suppression of indigenous culture by the dominant Catholic tradition, and when, in the 1980s, indigenous theologians put forward their own cultural and political claims in the Latin American church and beyond. It was also revealed in the conflicts between women's movements and the leaderships of liberation movements. Women who were initially part of the collective endeavour for economic liberation are now insisting that women's experiences be taken into account in a way that recognises their unique contribution to liberation theology.

Feminist interpretations of power

Different descriptions of power, for example 'power with' and 'power in relation' — rather than 'power over' — emerging from feminist theology, corresponded to ways that Latin American theologians might have talked about their practical politics. Likewise, the connections between military, economic, ecological and sexual violence and their effect on the lives of women and poor communities, the theme of a December 1994 dialogue between women theologians from North and South in Costa Rica, offered liberation theologians helpful connections between different forms of domination.

The phrases 'accompanying the poor' and 'empowerment' are key in the language of liberation theologians. They are not dissimilar to ways of looking at power circulating amongst feminist theologians such as Rosemary Ruether, Virginia Fabella and Tina Beattie. For all of these, some re-interpretation of the significance and nature ascribed by the Bible to the person of Mary, the Mother of Jesus, has been an implicit or explicit result. From this have come new ideas of power as nurture, and as a challenge to all forms of violence and domination.

Women's liberation

The events of 1989 led to a precipitous rush by communist-influenced parties into different, often opportunist and authoritarian, forms of social democracy, leaving behind traditionalist and dissident rumps. For many women in Central America this has been experienced as a profound betrayal. Having borne the brunt of guerrilla wars in which a party line dictated the suppression of women's issues, supposedly for the greater good and purity of class purpose in the national democratic struggle, they have watched the goalposts change, apparently in order that male leaderships can retain power. The lesson has been learnt both in base Christian communities and in broader political coalitions. The discrediting of the rhetoric of 'national democratic liberation struggles' has thus brought women's liberation to the fore. This has inevitably informed debate on the new agenda for liberation theology.

It used to be the normal thing for us to see what was the party line to follow, but if your work for any reason led you to do something else, then you were not following the party line any more [. . .] I think we women were the first to rebel against this style of exercising power, each of us in our own situation. Then we started to share our rebelliousness and to discover that the way in which the system is organised, including the trade unions, the political parties and the church, is not helping our development or giving us strength for the things we want to do. Then some people were expelled from their party, or they lost their jobs.

A lot of people left and became independent [. . .] As Christians or as feminists, these independent women participate in many activities and take on responsibilities but, as we say here: 'They represent their own tapeworms', not any organisation. They want autonomy.

Source: Isabel Ascencio, a former Lutheran pastor from El Salvador, quoted in Best, Marigold and Hussey, Pamela, *Life out of Death. The feminine spirit in El Salvador*, CIIR, London, 1996.

CIIR Comment

Entrenched hierarchical opposition to their pastoral practice in the church, and the goals of some liberation movements to 'seize power', imposed power struggles on the liberation theologians. Thus, conflicts about 'power over' people distorted alternative visions. It was only after the tacit truce with Rome in the late 1980s, and once liberation movements had entered into national peace processes, that such conflicts declined in intensity. This has permitted a more fruitful dialogue between liberation and feminist theology.

Ecology and eco-feminism

The philosophical underpinning of liberation theology is that knowledge is won from action, praxis. But, stemming from Christian tradition, this must be obedient action, obedient to God and revealed truth. A vital theme of religious obedience today is found in the realm of the integrity of creation, called by Christian and Biblical tradition 'stewardship' or, in Greek, *oikonomia*. Christians are thereby required to care for God's creation.

The ecological threat to humanity from industrialisation and human economic activity has become widely acknowledged in the past 25 years, particularly among feminist theologians. It is an urgent challenge to Christianity. A damaged planet will not sustain human life. The main themes of eco-feminism are expressed in the words of one theologian:

the demand is liberation: the emphasis is connectedness;
the corrective is suffering; the power is imagination; and
the vocation is *tikkun'olam* — the repair of the world.

Christian ecological concern is related to the tradition of love for the poor, for example in Franciscan spirituality. However, it carries imperatives that are not readily derived from the principle of liberation as the sole organising theological concept. Efficient, economic use of scarce resources like non-renewable energy is a good example. The poor are often the first to suffer from environmental degradation. But does obedient action on behalf of the poor always dovetail with obedient action on behalf of the integrity of creation? If not, how can these two traditions within Christian theology be reconciled? And what might the synthesis look like?

This question arises acutely in relation to the discrediting of socialism. One of the most telling revelations in the aftermath of the fall of the Berlin Wall was the extent of environmental degradation tolerated by communist regimes in the interests of industrialisation. Much of eastern Europe and the old Soviet Union had been literally poisoned in the arms and technology race with the United States. It is difficult to imagine how any criticism of this process could originate in the corpus of liberation theology during the 1980s. (This is not, of course, to deny that similar levels of irresponsibility characterised much of the liberal capitalist world during the same period.)

Nor does the question of stewardship challenge liberation theology alone. Vatican theology has hardly yet come to grips with Christian complicity in human domination of nature. Christian ecological concerns need to be assimilated into the option for the poor in a broader understanding of obedient action; the task is already engaging theologians across confessional boundaries.

Evangelical sects
It might be argued that as far as the rapid worldwide rise of the smaller evangelical churches was concerned, both Rome and the liberation theologians were caught off guard. Perhaps the most telling challenge to liberation theology has been people's rejection of base Christian communities, and indeed the Catholic church as a whole, in favour of evangelical and

pentecostal churches. For example, between 1990 and 1992, 710 new churches were formed in Sao Paolo, Brazil, and 91 per cent of these were pentecostal. The recent great missionary wave, originating in California, has created churches which have, on the whole, diverted Christians from the struggle for justice, from prophetic theology and from contesting the established order. Instead they have adapted converts for new roles in the neo-liberal dispensation through sponsoring values such as sobriety, punctuality, loyalty and cleanliness, as well as new forms of worship.

For a long time the 'sects' were discounted by the radical church as — at least in part — deliberate attempts to subvert the goals of liberation theology. But it became apparent that they also represented a genuine religious threat to both conservative and radical Catholics.

Today liberation theologians are discussing the issues raised by the doubling of the numbers of evangelical religious communities in the 1980s. The fundamental question is whether liberation theology took the religious context seriously enough in dealing with popular manifestations of faith. 'We ought to analyse not only the needs of the poor, but also their particular faith, which supplies the light by which they do theology,' Jon Sobrino wrote in 1995 in his preface to *Systematic Theology*.[10]

Another important question is whether liberation theology will be capable of dealing with questions of faith and meaning that face the poor in the context of a future secular and increasingly urban world. After all, the 'sects' represent a growing reaction to this world.

Secular consumerism

One area where conservative reaction to liberation theology might have been pointing in the right direction was its assertion that the growth of a secular, consumer society warrants the church's concern. Liberation theologians repudiated this as a theological problem for the North only, a diversion from the real issue of the idolatry of power and profit within the political economy.

Evangelical religion is often seen as the retrieval of the spiritual from the political contamination of Catholicism. Yet some now suggest that it might, in Latin America, turn out to be little more than a half-way house to consumerism and secularism. Liberation theology might thus need to take the preoccupations of Northern theology more seriously in future if it is to respect the context of urban life. This is not the only area where liberation theologians are setting out a new agenda on the basis of a process of self-criticism, but it is the one where the preoccupations of Rome are most accommodated.

From conflict to synthesis

There is a wider sense in which liberation theology is now handling conflict adroitly and has met Roman theology coming from the opposite direction after the clashes of the 1980s. For example, the personal-spiritual meaning to salvation given by Rome links with the social-political emphasis of liberation theology. As Leonardo Boff's brother, Clodovis Boff, wrote in *Systematic Theology*, the Vatican

> transformed the notion of liberation into a great notion that embraces the whole mystery of salvation [. . .] it starts with liberation [. . .] from sin and death and from there moves to the social dimension [liberation from historical oppression]. In this wise, Rome arrives at ethico-social liberation, while Latin American liberation theology arrives at [liberation from personal sin and death].

It is true that liberation theology initially failed in not coming to grips with feminism, ecology, the evangelical sects and what the Cambridge school describes as the violence inherent in political thought. Yet this failure needs to be set against its abiding achievements. These are to have recuperated a sense of the gospel as comprehensively political, and to have defined theology as concerned with life, not simply with a narrow and private domain of 'privatised religion'.

The new agenda

The remorseless propaganda used against liberation theology since its inception was designed to damn it by association with communism and socialism. Because of this, the collapse of communism in Eastern Europe after 1989 and the subsequent dismemberment of the Soviet Union were interpreted by its opponents as the death-knell for liberation theology.

Nonetheless, the links between some liberation theologians and political movements of the left did not provide adequate grounds for proclaiming the collapse of a theology that sought its legitimacy in biblical texts and from the experience and faith of the poor. The epoch-making events that, to use historian Eric Hobsbawm's phrase, brought the 'short 20th century' to an end in 1991, did not bring an end to the oppression of the poor. Nor was the global assimilation of liberation theology themes into church life a sign of it being a burnt-out case.

Post-modernism and a time for reflection
Liberation theology opened itself up to widespread condemnation by using analysis based on sociological theories that

were eminently falsifiable and inadequate. But that hardly accounted for the widespread demoralisation and loss of nerve that struck the left and extended to radical Christians in the early 1990s. This was perhaps less to do with the demise of a 'really existing socialism' (in which virtually no one — including most of its advocates — believed) than with the growing penetration of post-modern thought. This tends towards a repudiation of any broad political frameworks and traditions, together with grand stories, or 'meta-narratives', about the meaning and direction of human history.

Post-modernism had imperceptibly gained ground during the 1980s, seeping into arguments about the fabric of society and into the assumptions of popular political discourse. It strove to demolish coercive grand stories with utopian endings in favour of pluralism and cultural relativism. Liberation theology looked like two grand stories caught in bed together — socialism and Christianity.

At another level, the elimination of the alternative eastern bloc economic system — despite its obvious defects — seemed more the end of a book than the closing of a chapter. It appeared to spell an end to all alternatives to global capitalism. The premise of liberation theology that things could be otherwise for the poor could no longer be validated from the secular political and economic alternatives on offer. There were none that plausibly promised to conquer poverty and injustice. The Enlightenment idea of linear progress which perhaps, as the Cambridge critics assert, once whistled through the superstructure of liberation theology, had vanished. The left was becalmed.

So, for those who saw liberation theology mainly as an attractive novelty, now may be the moment to move on to the next theological fashion. But for those who see themselves as part of a movement that is barely 25 years old, and which has lived with the urgency of dire poverty for all these years, a temporary becalming of the left may be no bad thing. There is no fit between theological analysis and the programmes of particular political parties today. An uncritical leap from one to the other, so tempting, is always likely to be wrong. An engagement with different experiences of poverty, though, remains as the springboard to political action, the rock on which liberation theology will build its church.

The present situation therefore offers the opportunity for liberation theology to adopt a much more self-critical stance before it moves forward. This does not mean abandoning the fundamental insights of its methodology: reading the signs of the times in the context of the preferential option for the poor; analysing the sources of alienation and oppression; and seeking knowledge through action for change. As the liberation theologians emphasise, this means building into a wider analysis the various kinds of oppression, not simply socio-economic forms, 'but also those perpetrated in the areas of culture, ethnicity, religion, women, children and nature', to use Jon Sobrino's words in *Systematic Theology*.[11]

Who are 'the poor'?

Liberation theology is widening its concept of 'the poor' and looking at different cultures with a renewed seriousness. The enormous challenges of taking 'the other' seriously, whether in the context of gender, ethnicity or religion, are seen as a necessary part of reading the signs of the times. True, this emphasis might also be viewed as borrowing from the post-modern dissolution of grand narratives. It might also suggest that liberation theology will henceforth not look at the whole picture because such a picture does not exist.

However, in a globalised economy liberation theology cannot allow itself to be deprived of a universal critique. The structures of domination that oppress the poor today require that liberation theology seek a concrete, not abstract universality, and become more universalist and internationalist at the same time as becoming more differentiated, local and rigorous.

Being more rigorous about who are 'the poor' has long been acknowledged by liberation theology as one of its tasks. The danger is that this will end in a fragmentation and provincialisation of its vision. Despite organisations such as EATWOT and initiatives such as the Damascus document, there has been no 'Christian International' movement clustered around liberation theologians as intellectual leaders, and little truly internationalist action and analysis. The different liberation theologies have been national, provincial and rarely more than regional in the scope of their analysis.

Shared international predicament

Nonetheless, the international relations of exploitation, violence and injustice, and the overarching ideologies of the World Trade Organisation, international financial institutions and transnational corporations, demand that the concept of what is 'contextual' be widened to root it in the contemporary global economy. The neo-liberalism of which the bishops of Latin America spoke in Santo Domingo in 1992 had its impact no less in Africa, Asia and Europe. The speed and magnitude of capital flows, the internationalisation of production, and the rapid impoverishment of certain regions such as Africa, and development of others such as the Pacific Rim, give a new configuration to poverty. Given that some 800 million people go hungry daily even in the midst of today's communications revolution, the sheer scale of socio-economic poverty should call into question any provincial concept of context, and any radical rupture with liberation theology's original focus.

Christians, North and South, face a common agenda deriving from a shared predicament. This is what the *New Testament* called 'the world', 'the principalities and powers'; today it might be called the global structures of sin and complex connections that bind people into relationships of complicity. Systematic and effective strategies of resistance can only arise out of analyses of these international conditions. These will need to be more refined than those first used by liberation theology. Mounting any Christian challenge to these international relations will require a far greater insistence that the voices of the excluded and marginalised are heard directly, rather than ventriloquised through an international — clerical — élite.

The question which poses itself is whether any isolated Christian response in a pluralist world can be adequate? Should we leave behind the self-preoccupations of Christian churches for a shared ecumenical concern with non-Christians committed to liberation?

Liberation in other religious traditions

Any religious tradition may become involved in an option for the poor and, as a second step, reflect on it in the light of its spiritual insights, themes and doctrines. The critical factor is, of course, the experience of oppression and a historical consciousness of domination. The principle of liberation can come to play an important role even in primal religions that lack sacred texts.

Priests at the Mwari Cult shrine in Zimbabwe's Matopos Hills, for example, supported the liberation struggle in the war for land and, more recently, instructed cult-followers in oracular utterances to plant trees. The war would be lost if the soil was eroded and the land made barren. Mwari wanted fertile land for the good of the Zimbabwean people and recognised that action had to be taken if the process of liberation were not to founder. The Mwari oracle probably would not have distinguished between 'stewardship' and 'the option for the poor', even if it had absorbed such Christian terms from the churches around.

In religious systems with sacred texts the generation of a distinct liberation theology depends on a re-reading of the texts in the light of an option for the poor. In other words, it means applying hermeneutics — the art of interpreting, for a contemporary context, texts or symbols from a past or distant culture. A disciplined act of interpreting a text means acknowledging complex differences in the horizons and expectations of its authors and readers.

Muslim experiences of liberation theology

Islam has traditionally understood the Holy Qur'an as the

direct utterance of God, spoken to his prophet, Muhammad, 'in the purest Arabic'. It operates with different hermeneutic principles from those familiar to Western scholars. Nonetheless, Islamic writers in a number of different countries have begun to elaborate a Muslim liberation theology and to grapple with the Qur'anic text in this endeavour. Such writers need, of course, to be distinguished from radical Muslims whose primary horizon is a revolutionary transformation of society away from pluralism towards a traditional Islamic theology and rigid application of *Shari'a* Law.

The South African Muslim, Farid Esack, takes as his theme 'inter-religious solidarity against oppression'. Esack himself was closely involved in the South African liberation struggle and was imprisoned on a number of occasions for his political work and anti-apartheid stance. As such he is an exponent of the action-reflection-action cycle and liberation theology methodology. He points to a number of key Qur'anic words: *tawhid* ('divine unity'); *al-nas* ('the people'); *al-mustad'afun fi'l-ard* ('the oppressed of the earth'); *adl* and *qist* ('balance' and 'justice'); and *jihad* ('struggle and praxis'). After grappling with the problem of hermeneutics from a Muslim perspective, he relates these themes to the experience of South African Muslims in the national liberation struggle, particularly in the 1980s.

Farid Esack shares with Asghar Ali Engineer of the Institute of Islamic Studies in Bombay, India, and some other radical Muslims in Asia, a profound concern to overcome traditional Muslim prohibitions against forming alliances with Christians, Jews and Hindus. He sets this ban in the context of relationships with the 'unjust and unrighteous Other and not solidarity with the exploited and marginalised Other'. The seminal concept of *tawhid* is broadened to imply the unity of humankind and a rejection of interpretations of the Qur'an that accommodate class division. A *tawhidi* society would be a

Utopia involving no class or other divisions. This theme characterised the thought of the Muslim scholar Ali Shari'ati and the Iranian Mujahidin-I-Khalq movement.

Farid Esack's liberation theology thus seeks to overcome the exclusion implied by the concept of *kufr* (unbelief) by a process of re-interpretation. He points to one of the *Meccan Surahs* (chapters in the Qur'an) as most suggestive of the core content of belief and unbelief:

> Have you observed him who belies the religious? It is he who turns away the orphan and does not urge others to feed the poor. Woe to those who pray but are heedless in their prayer; who make a show of piety and obstruct the needy from necessities. (Qur'an 107.)

The corollary in the Qur'anic texts is that the *mustad'afun* (the oppressed) for whom God unambiguously takes a preferential option in a section called *al-Qasas* (the story) are distinguished from *mustakbirun* (the powerful and arrogant) even though the former may not be Muslim.

Need for analysis and cultural appraisal

As Farid Esack's primary preoccupations illustrate, liberation theology arising in oppressive societies in which a number of different religious traditions coexist has to solve difficulties of solidarity across confessional boundaries. But due consideration of religious difference is also basic to any thoroughgoing liberationist approach. Felix Wilfred, writing as a Christian theologian from an Indian experience, for example, sets up the hope that by becoming involved in the process of liberation

> the church community will realise the action of God in the wider world, in other religions, and in the signs of the times, and thereby arrive at a nuancing and certain relativisation of its absolute claims.[12]

This Asian emphasis on religious pluralism, however, has its inherent difficulties. This is particularly true of the Indian case where liberation theology examines Indian society from the perspective of the Dalits. For India's Dalits, known formerly as untouchables, any immersion in popular Hindu religiosity raises questions about how much Hinduism is responsible for the legitimisation of the caste system which excludes them.

The problems do not end there. For Rome today the new dragon to be slain is cultural and religious relativism. The degree of assimilation of other religious themes and the level of 'relativisation' found in the works of Tissa Balasuriya,[13] the Sri Lankan theologian, helped bring about his excommunication in 1996.

Whether it is cooperation with radical Buddhist groups in South East Asia,[14] or coming to terms with indigenous religious thought in the Andes, the option for the poor in plural societies requires a demanding and critical analysis and appraisal of culture. As the work of Farid Esack illustrates, solidarity in a common liberation struggle both demands and stimulates this discernment.

Conclusion

The idea that liberation theology suffered an irreversible decline after 1989 was an illusion of perspective. The enemies of liberation theology had inflated the numerical importance and politicisation of basic Christian communities at the apogee of the Cold War in the 1980s, and made an effective propaganda claim that equated liberation theology with Marxist infiltration of the church. This made the fall of the Berlin Wall look like the beginning of a terminal decline in Christian radicalism around the world.

The truth was different. The fundamental tenets of liberation theology's methods had — almost surreptitiously — been broadly accepted in many parts of the Catholic church. It had entered the spiritual bloodstream of many churches. For many Christians it renewed their spirituality and gave them a new sense of what the Christian life might mean in the modern world. An awareness that theology should not be done without reference to the situation in which people live, and that the defining theological characteristic of that context is the action of God in and through the lives of the poor, is part of the air which a significant section of the Catholic vanguard breathes today. This has brought immense changes.

For a critical period, from 1968 to 1992, while it became established in the church, liberation theology provided the theology and then the spirituality to underpin the church's option for the poor. It will continue to do so, despite entrenched opposition, but it will no longer hit the headlines. For the poor, in their invisibility and insignificance, now live in 'ordinary' not revolutionary times. Liberation theology is evolving with questions about culture, feminism and ecology to the fore. Consumerism, secularism and religious pluralism are being broached as fundamental issues for an effective understanding of an option for the poor. The exploration of all these themes carries great risks of censure and diversion but also great opportunities for the poor to 'speak truth to power'.

The insights that informed liberation theology's contribution to development — the inevitability of conflict with élites, the priority of the experience of the grassroots and the analysis of local structures of domination — remain no less valid today. Liberation theology still contests the dominant model of development in which poor people are treated as the collateral damage of advanced capitalism. Likewise, it still attracts Christians whose spiritual journey begins with an option for the poor, who wish to work for justice and development, and who may doubt whether the Vatican has seriously taken the same option, whatever the fine words of papal encyclicals.

Today, Christian work for justice needs more urgently than ever the evangelisation rather than the abandonment of the political. It still demands that those lumped under the title 'the poor' be heard and understood. In the face of globalisation, it calls out for a politics, an economics and a society in which people can live with human dignity, liberated from destitution.

The magnitude of this task, which has not diminished with the end of the 20th century, means that Christians North and South will need to embrace like-minded people. By sharing strategies they will have to join in a common pursuit of international economic justice. Through this common pursuit people will discover, propose and enact structures and forms of power and politics which exhibit 'the peaceable generosity of God'. Out of this ecumenical endeavour, the contours of the liberation theology of the next century will emerge. Liberation theology has come of age, but it is early days yet.

Notes

1. Gutiérrez, G, *A Theology of Liberation*, Orbis, New York, 1973.

2. *The Medellín Statement of the Bishops of Latin America*, New Blackfriars, Oxford, November 1968.

3. *Ibid.*

4. Penny Lernoux estimates that about 1,000 bishops, priests and nuns were murdered in Latin America for political reasons between 1964 and 1980. See Lernoux, Penny, *Cry of the People*, Penguin, London/New York, 1982.

5. *Puebla Conclusions. Evangelisation at Present and in the Future.* No.1134, CIIR, London, 1980.

6. *Instruction on Certain Aspects of the Theology of Liberation*, Congregation for the Doctrine of the Faith, Vatican, September 1984.

7. Boff, Leonardo, *Church: Charism and Power*, SCM, London 1985.

8. *Instruction on Christian Freedom and Liberation*, Congregation for the Doctrine of the Faith, Vatican, March 1986.

9. *Message of John Paul II to the Episcopate of Brazil*, Congregation for the Doctrine of the Faith, Vatican, 9 April 1986.

10. Sobrino, Jon and Ellacuria, Ignacio, *Systematic Theology*, Orbis, New York, 1996.

11. *Ibid.*

12. Wilfred, Felix,'Action Groups and the Struggle for Justice in India', *Ecumenical Review* 1987, 39/3.

13. Balasuriya, Tissa, *Mary and Human Liberation*, Cassell, London, 1991.

14. Amaladoss, M, *Life in Freedom: Liberation Theologies from Asia*, Maryknoll, New York, 1997, gives a comprehensive view of Asian liberation theologies.

Key texts

Beattie, T, *Rediscovering Mary: Insights from the Gospels*, Burns & Oates, London 1995.

Berryman, Phillip, *Liberation Theology. The Essential Facts about the Revolutionary Movement in Latin America and Beyond*, Pantheon Books, New York, 1987.

Best, Marigold and Hussey, Pamela, *Life out of Death. The Feminine Spirit in El Salvador*, CIIR, London, 1996.

Boff, Leonardo, *Jesus Christ Liberator*, Orbis, New York, 1978.

CIIR/British Council of Churches, *The Kairos Document. Challenge to the Church. A Theological Comment on the Political Crisis in South Africa*, London, 1985.

CIIR/Christian Aid, *The Road to Damascus: Kairos and Conversion*, London, 1989.

de la Torre, Ed, *Touching Ground, Taking Root. Theological and Political Reflections on the Philippine Struggle*, CIIR/British Council of Churches, London, 1986.

Fabella, Virginia, *Beyond Bonding: A Third World Women's Theological Journey*, EATWOT/Institute of Women's Studies, Manila, 1973.

Gutiérrez, Gustavo, *A Theology of Liberation*, Orbis, New York, 1973.

King, Ursula, *Feminist Theology from the Third World. A Reader*, SPCK, London, 1994.

Lash, Nicholas, 'Not Exactly Politics or Power?', in *Modern Theology* Vol. 8, No. 4, October 1992.

Lernoux, Penny, *Cry of the People. United States Involvement in the Rise of Fascism, Torture, and Murder and the Persecution of the Church in Latin America*, Penguin, London/New York, 1982.

Milbank, John, *Theology and Social Theory — Beyond Secular Reason*, Oxford University Press, Oxford, 1990.

New Blackfriars, *A Theology of Liberation Twenty Years On*, Oxford, October 1991.

Ratzinger, Joseph, 'Central Problem for Faith', in *Briefing*, Vol. 27, 16 January 1997.

Ruether, RR, *Women-Church: Theology and Practice*, Harper & Row, New York, 1985.

Sobrino, Jon, *Companions of Jesus: The Murder and Martyrdom of the Salvadorean Jesuits*, CIIR, London 1990.

Sobrino, Jon and Ellacuria, Ignacio, *Systematic Theology*, Orbis, New York, 1996.

Tamez, E, *Women's Theology from Latin America*, Orbis, New York, 1989.

Turner, D, *Marxism and Christianity*, Blackwell, Oxford, 1983.

The **Catholic Institute for International Relations (CIIR)** works to overcome poverty and injustice in the Third World. Founded in 1940, it is an independent charity which works with people of any religious belief or none. CIIR's **International Policy Department** carries out research, analysis, advocacy and development education on democracy, human rights, peace processes and international economic justice in Asia, Latin America, the Caribbean and Southern Africa.

International Cooperation for Development (ICD), CIIR's overseas department, recruits experienced professionals to share their skills in development projects in Latin America and the Caribbean, Africa and the Middle East.

CIIR has consultative status at the Economic and Social Council of the United Nations (ECOSOC)
Charity registration no. 294329.

Members of CIIR receive *CIIR News*, the Institute's *Annual Review* and booklets in the *Comment* series. Members are also invited to CIIR international conferences and offered special discounts on a range of new books. Annual subscription rates are: UK £15; unwaged £5; overseas £20.

For further information on membership or publications, please contact:

CIIR, Unit 3 Canonbury Yard,
190a New North Road, London N1 7BJ, UK
Tel 0171 354 0883. International +44 171 354 0883
Fax 0171 359 0017. International +44 171 359 0017
E-mail: ciir@ciir.org